THE SECRET TO LIFE'S

BANK

ISBN-13: 978-1522776925

ISBN-10: 1522776923

NOTICE TO OUR READERS

The Publisher has strived to be as accurate and complete as possible in the creation of this book, notwithstanding the fact that he does not warrant or represent at any time that the contents within are accurate due to the rapidly changing nature of the Internet.

This book is a common sense guide to pursuing wealth. In practical advice books, like anything else in life, there are no guarantees of income made. Readers are cautioned to reply on their own judgment about their individual circumstances to act accordingly.

This book is not intended for use as a source of legal, business, accounting or financial advice. All readers are advised to seek services of competent professionals in legal, business, accounting, and finance field.

Any perceived slights of specific people or organizations are unintentional.

Table of Contents

This book is designed to meet the requirements of people who desire of achieving greater heights by implementing very simple and yet powerful concepts that have the potential to change your life completely.

It is not intended to be a book based on hypothetical research nor is it a philosophical treatise, but it is a book that uncovers information that will bring a lasting incentive allowing us to unleash the inner resources of strength and dynamic willpower to the fore.

In fact it is a compilation of facts presented in simple layman's English and contains information that is going to bring immense joy and success in your life.

It covers profound and dynamic truths conveyed in few potent words that kindle a renewed sense of awareness of our limitless latent inner resources waiting to burst into the open. It comprises practical expressions that have the potential to bring success, health, wealth and enduring happiness.

One of the most difficult points to reconcile in life is the paradox that suffering exists in this world. Suffering is eminent.

Of course, what is equally important is realizing that the acquisition and possession of wealth is not a ruler that measures one's happiness. If joy truly were to be found in materials, then all those who experience the 'thrill' of it by coming into contact with the object would observe the same measure of joy.

In life, people are continuously motivated by two inevitable impulses of repulsion – from sorrow and craving to seeking joy and absolute fulfillment. In the quest to embrace all happiness, they are compelled to run after the enjoyable and agreeable, while confronting the opposites, they avoid undesirable objects and disagreeable environments.

The fact is this: throughout history, all achievers conscious or subconsciously have used six principles, which are common to absolute progress in all aspects of life.

The 6 Virtues to Unlocking Success

These virtues are a key to unlocking amazing cache of wealth, abundance and success. They are all centered on our true innate qualities, which as a matter of fact are universal and have a spiritual basis. These virtues are:

- Truth
- Righteousness
- Peace
- Love
- Non-violence

- Forgiveness

The practice of these virtues will enable anyone to progress in life without any doubt.

The reason is simple.

These universal virtues are all attractive and needless to say, they form the cornerstones of the code of ethics. You cannot go wrong practicing the importance to moral values, codes of conduct and obeying the Law of Nature in your pursuit of Wealth.

In the coming pages, you will discover the goal of reaching financial freedom while at the same time, acquiring the perfect art of happiness through the understanding that *the measure of joy is not 'directly' proportional to just monetary wealth.*

This concise, precise and straight-to-the-point manuscript explores avenues that are most definitely going to change your life for the better.

Unlike many other books on the same subject, this manuscript delves on subject areas relevant to aspects of your personal life and growth that I can guarantee will bring back that smile on your face. It is clear, focused and above all a readable book, which you will enjoy.

It Can Never Happen?

While pessimism warns us of dangers lurking before our very own eyes, optimism may propel us into false security. Pessimism should only be considered initial and not a final predicament in any situation – this is the **first step** to success.

Time and again, we have been subjected to instances that are disturbing, and deep within us we 'realize' the potential dangers and risks surrounding us, and the 'voice' within adamantly rejects this threatening situation confronting us, as such because we fail to recognize this 'voice' within us our mental clinging to the outer world detaches us from the inner voice of 'TRUTH' thereby throwing us totally of the tracks as it were.

The **second step** to success and wealth is to convince yourself of the importance of self-control, self-awareness and self-discipline.

We must listen to the voice within and realize the existence of the innate force or the Dynamic Willpower – the mighty power expressing through the mind, body and the intellect! Thus the second step qualifies that you develop faith in not just what you can do and achieve but most importantly developing faith in yourself (your innate, inherent and latent qualities).

Step three requires that through constant vigilance, employing the power of intelligence, self analysis and introspection and through careful understanding and use of these concepts, you can learn to live beyond the demands of the mind in whatever environment you find yourself – this will qualify you to implement and embrace the road to wealth.

There is no such thing as a free lunch. If you hate to put in any work/effort but love to attain success, you will have to reconsider your views.

So to achieve the latter, you have to do the former. <u>The sensible idea is to find out what really gives us pleasure and then find out if it is possible to make money from doing it.</u>

"If you do not start you will not succeed."

Pursuing Wealth

The statement 'haste makes waste' stands true even today, and more often than not, some of us tend to feel frustrated when we cannot live up to our ideals and the standards we set for ourselves all the time.

On other occasions, we may feel that had we taken the challenge that came our way that perhaps things may well have changed for the better, yet there is also the possibility that in our over anxiety to reach the goal we try too hard and burn ourselves out entirely!

Has This Happened to You?

The question that now remains to be asked how do we begin, how can we achieve success in life?

Well, my friend, rest assured that this book has been written to answer this question satisfactorily, eliminating confusion or anomalies whatsoever.

There are many strategies that one can employ and various means through which you can plough yourself to achieving the goal. One common thread in all of them is self-belief, self-righteousness or honesty, and ethical living (in words, deeds, thoughts and actions) pertaining to your lifestyle – this is **Step four**.

In any business the emphasis on moral and ethical standards ranks the highest, and this should not be ignored or overlooked.

The only way to achieve equanimity, balance or equilibrium even after you become the wealthiest individual is to have your sense of realizing the true essence of life.

Nothing in life is constant. Life is ever changing and things that seem to have existence today may cease to exist tomorrow and this is a fact that you – and everyone else – must learn to accept.

Step five, when you discover something profound and beautiful, the natural tendency is to share it with others.

In the following chapters what you will discover are the true ways to achieve complete success, and this is a book that will allow you to unleash your innate qualities to the fore, thereby allowing you to reap the benefits and the rewards that thousands of people all over the world at this very second are enjoying because they have become wealthy.

Follow the guide within the coming pages, fore it is my sincere believe that every person has the potential to succeed in life.

"Wealth is more than just money."

It is the privilege of the human race to achieve all around greatness, and in reality success should be one's habit. People are essentially perfect, and therefore infinite are the possibilities that lie dormant within them.

In order to bring out the very best from within, a life organized and perfectly disciplined for the discovery of the potentialities that lie lurking within us, is a life well spent.

The vital point is not how many talents each one of us has, but the importance should be focused on how much of our existing talents, attributes and capabilities are we prepared to explore, develop, exploit, and implement in our daily lives.

The question you must ask, is whether you are making a practical use of at least one great talent lying inherent within you? *The one supreme fundamental principal is to understand that all our success entirely depends upon ourselves.*

The best way to be happy is to do the things that you naturally love and enjoy doing – something that you are absolutely passionate about! Likewise the best way to succeed and become wealthy is to see to it that you achieve the things you have earnestly desired to seek in life. This will require that you implement your efforts in to activities that will allow you to measure success.

For instance the simple way to explain this is to take into consideration the following example: if you take a liking for art, painting, and drawing then the way to proceed is to seek guidance on ways to enter competitions, and ways to submit your artwork via galleries (approach galleries directly and leave work on a sale or return basis) or fine art publishers' or even exposing your talent by entering seasonal fairs where you will find a large gathering of all kinds of retailers.

You may want to add various different types of themes to your art portfolio in order to maximize your capabilities to reach an audience far and wide with interests in different themes/subjects.

Contact groups, forums and even Internet newsgroups and explore various other avenues (such as photographers, photo and framing galleries, arts councils and government organizations that provide help including loans etc.) that will allow you to step up your enquiry – the idea is to pursue the goal relentlessly and with a positive attitude.

As far as your theme/subject matter is concerned post questions, polls, surveys, and determines what people are looking for, and then simply find the need and fill it.

Every little will help, but it is the force required to get the momentum going and that is the key point. Another useful point is not to just try, try and to continue trying – instead develop an attitude whereby you DO the thing you have decided to pursue, implement and apply the strategies shown in this book.

Finally do not just stop at that – keep faith and do not yield to any defeat. Once you have decided to put the 'plan' into action, make sure that it is kept ignited and glowing…rejections and disappointments should in no way curtail your hope, progress and your desire to success. People who have succeeded despite all the hardship, pain and struggle have inspired countless millions around the world – it is time you too set an example for others to follow in your footsteps.

You must remember that the methods employed by different individuals in procuring wealth may be distinct, but the goal is common to all, and the steps spoken of earlier are in effect your tools to your overall success.

Very strong willpower is needed in order to develop internally, and the need for two most important attributes, namely courage and confidence are essential ingredients. Thus poverty and prosperity does not necessarily depend on knowledge wholly (e.g. business acumen, marketing strategies and so on) but it certainly depends on the three C's and they are character, creativity and your innate capabilities.

Courage and confidence alone can bring about unique transformation while the opposite will only bring much sorrow and despair in times of distress and crisis. However, despite life's problems we should resist obstacles and hindrances and as such constantly remind ourselves of the supreme inherent or innate power which we all posses and which we can all successfully develop through spiritual insight. Thus ignoring our abilities and potential for developing the personal power that we need for going through ego-breaking experiences requires immense fortitude and discipline, and I explain to you in this book on how you could achieve all this here and now.

Without these qualities you are destined to fail, and that is the reason why a large portion of people feel despondent because they got into competition or they simply gave up under pressure, through lack of self-courage and dynamic willpower.

When our fantasies and expectations are not fulfilled, there is a tendency for us to revert to our old ways – the hollowness we experience can be most annoying and we cannot ignore it forever. A lot of the time what exactly happens is that whatever good we undertake in life, it does not mean we will continue. This is not because an impossible discipline is required but because we lack courage and confidence we are overwhelmed with negative attitude – this is what stops everything in its tracks!

The initial burst of enthusiasm begins to fade, and what seemed so wonderful becomes a peril a dilemma and a problem. The mind takes over and questions surmount raising doubts after doubts whether the whole idea or concept is worthwhile – a conflict ensues, the mind says the one thing and the intellect and our intuition urges us to follow the path to 'success'.

Even before we begin the journey the end is imminent, because we are undecided what true path to follow. Success lies in what you make of it not what you 'think' it ought to be (do not fantasize success).

So how can we get started?

Formula to Success

What you think and how you then act is the deciding factor that will help you discover the goal of success. These two attributes are important together with a set of consistent principles, which you follow through. Thoughts based on reason are a powerful catalyst to start any reaction, and once you set off, you will soon realize that courage is the simple virtue needed for a human being to traverse the rocky road.

Obstacles are natural, and they are a means to the source of acquiring wealth, as I am sure you will agree. Persistence, patience and perseverance will have to be practiced religiously to reach the goal and to overcome the obstacles. Of course that said, I would now like to point out the P's that you should frown upon.

Do not **procrastinate**, do not **pretend** that you know it all and finally do not **prolong** your 'venture(s)'. Be prepared to fight the stumbling blocks that may confront you, but pursue your goal and allow your potential willpower to predominate.

In any situation in life, it is unequivocally important to remain level headed, despite all the 'ups and the downs' that we are likely to face. Remember life is dualistic by nature – the obverse and the reverse sides of the same coin to put it simply. I am compelled to add that though we know that the past is the cause and the present is the effect, it is self evident that with time the present itself becomes the cause with reference to the future.

There is a very deep meaning embroiled in this syntax, and if you can relate this to success, then it can be said that if we intelligently live in the scientific self-discipline, we can become the architects of our own future.

The Basic Steps

The following guidelines will help you pave a wonderful path to your ultimate success.

The steps are very simple to implement in your daily life.

1. Do what you love and what you are good at.

2. Be prepared to learn and to be positive (motivation and enthusiasm).

3. Be an innovative individual.

4. Be prepared to invest not just money but your time, effort and resources, too.

I mentioned money – this does not mean that you have to invest a large sum to become a millionaire or wealthy.

5. You must be disciplined in having set goals and targets. Remember that persistence is the key to success.

6. You must be prepared to manage your time effectively.

7. As you evolve, learn to give back what you amass to the society. I call this philanthropy.

You must have a solid vision – one in which you 'see' yourself having attained success. Great people of the past and present see to it that they reach this coveted position, by employing these basic steps.

However, notice in step 2 I deliberately used the word 'learn', and that too for a very good reason. Life is the greatest teacher, thus you must be willing to accept challenges all the time (using the power of discrimination) and thus as a result you must learn via its eternal principles the magnificent doctrine it has revealed with the passing of time. This means that you must act when the time is right.

Action is incredibly important and highlights success – the two are synonymous to be quite honest. To succeed action is needed but the essential ingredient is how serious you are. Being too serious can ruin your business venture, *so the point is to have FUN.*

Any discipline will require organization and orderliness. You must as I mentioned in the introduction be prepared to listen to your inner voice as much as you possibly can. This means that rather than being too dependent on your family, friends and so on (not that this is bad) begin to have faith in your own capabilities.

Stand-alone and strive to learn and succeed. Often, failures may just result from instances where we have stopped exercising our own views, or we have become too dependent on others'.

Success is not some secret that you have to search for or unearth in order to reach your destination; it is rather the understanding or the recognition factor that you develop with respect to what you really want in life. Intuition, courage, skills, knowledge, challenges and opportunities are some of the concepts that determine the traits of people who enjoy wealth. Any task performed with the right spirit will give you victory. Mental attitude is what will give you success, but negative attitude, laziness and working unwillingly will result in failure.

Do not expect too much in too short a time, but your approach should be positive and execute your task with absolute perfection, paying particular attention to your long-term goal(s). This means that you approach your duty with concentrated energy and you execute your plans righteously. This should be your philosophy of life.

To begin a new venture, it vitally important that you realize the following, which I have to say is crucial. You have to appreciate the fact that to start a business you need to acquaint yourself with the term cash flow. Investment in the form of a capital is a requirement, but more importantly it is the concept of viability of the business venture that matters most.

Steps to Personal Wealth

Decision-making is perhaps the hardest step to get over within your quest to begin the journey to wealth. The problem is until you do not delve deep within yourself to unlock your innate qualities chances are that you will be indecisive and hesitant. This is not wrong as such, but more often than not this 'feeling' may not allow you to maximize your full potential.

There is no secret to unleashing your full-blown potential – the 'secret' lies in your willingness to listen to your inner voice. The initiative to seize a good opportunity that comes your way is by undertaking the task in a methodical way.

Sit quietly, calm your senses and thoughts, and meditate deeply on the subject matter in question. Do not jump into anything at once just because the idea seems favorable. Most things appear very 'good' in the initial phase, but thinking, planning and time are a prerequisite. Often it is something within that will tell you what to do. The secret is not necessarily from without, but can be acquired from within.

Striving to do your very best at all times is the little secret that will help you amass wealth. Imagination (I mean constructive imagination) which is the power to visualize is an important factor in creative thought – but as you will appreciate you will not be able to do this without a strong will, and above all this faculty of visualization has to be ripened into firm belief and conviction.

1. You must have the desire to achieve your goal of fame – this is rule number one.

2. Be prepared to handle money efficiently with respect to budget, expenditure and responsibility and/or accountability.

3. Do not spend more than you are required to and spend less than you make.

4. Personal problems, including addiction not only to drugs etc., can be ruinous. This is something that must be taken care of from the very onset.

5. Figure out ways to invest and above all begin to save money. You will have to play smart and get your priorities absolutely right.

In any venture, it is likely that you may face a lot of antagonism, a far cry from an idealistic situation. Over expectations, over optimism and the tendency to 'wish' that things run as planned, can and often may lead to failure.

Thus as mentioned earlier planning is very important to your success. Of course the other factors that one needs to consider also are over work and exhaustion. In the hope to make your millions, the probability is that you will become a frustrated wreck and become quite despondent – this will not be helpful in your progress or pursuit to wealth.

Achieving Your Goal

When you persist refusing to accept failure, know that the object you have set out to achieve will materialize through the dynamic willpower.

Thoughts can be incredibly powerful tools, and if you are willing to implement this divine gift then you are sure to attain your goal. If you cling to a certain thought with dynamic willpower, it assumes a tangible outward form.

Now is the time to cauterize the negative characteristics inherent in the form of habits, lack of strong willpower, lack of confidence, hesitance and wrong attitude towards life in general. You have within you the power to accomplish everything you want, that power lies in the will. The root cause of failure in life is lack of concentration – do not hoard yourself with ideas, concepts and strategies all at once in the very hope to succeed. Begin slowly and be consistent in your goal setting scheme.

Focus your attention on one thing at a time, and do not allow your MIND to go in a state of 'over drive'. There is a scientific way of utilizing concentration, and the magic word is to keep calm, while you perform all your duties with the correct speed.

Do NOT rush and create chaos, but rather methodically and meticulously focus and centre your whole mind on whatever you undertake, and the important thing is to keep your mind flexible.

Once you know that you are genuinely on the right tracks and on the path to achieving your goal, do exercise care as far as time management is concerned. It is often very easy to get involved with a project so much so that you can get carried away in perfecting whatever it is that you are doing.

You must prioritize your work and above all respect and honor the value of time – do not waste your time and your life!

The Keys to Success

As I have mentioned the environment plays a huge role as it is quite inevitable – particularly our inner environment.

A calm relaxed individual is far more likely to come out a winner in a trying situation than his/her counterpart – a person who his nervous frustrated and erratic. The former has his senses fully identified with the environment in which he places himself.

However, the restless individual does not understand the environment and consequently gets into trouble. The keywords are focus, concentration and care in whatever you do in life.

1. Develop a definite and a clear-cut goal/aim.

2. Draw up a wise workable plan/program.

3. Guard your health. Without health there is no real wealth.

4. You must conserve your energy.

5. Be honest in your life (in words, deeds, thoughts and actions).

6. Stick to virtues and adopt good principles.

7. Reflect upon ideal personalities and seek strength from their philosophy.

8. Seek divine guidance and be truthful.

9. Endeavor to help and serve others with gratitude.

10. Always think positive and believe in the power of God.

Transformative thinking is indeed the way to success. Set out a plan to achieve your goal and deliberately ruminate over the meaning of this plan and make it happen.

From time immemorial great people from all walks of life have emerged as true victors and the reason behind this is training the mind for happiness. Ethical discipline is essential, particularly self-discipline.

Each individual is unique. What is good for person A may not be suitable for person B. However, it has to be emphasized that all can enjoy quietude, solitude and silence, and to be honest every individual irrespective of age, caste, creed, color, sex has at some stage or another experienced peace.

After discovering through trial and error method, you can determine the precise way to compose your mind body complex and thus attain great heights.

Meditation may not be effective for all, but that does not mean that you do not improvise such methods as and when required.

Be systematic, and your only goal should be to employ methods that bring you success and happiness.

Our mental faculties determine our actions, and it is quite obvious that the mind should be tamed and subdued. Constant vigilance is necessary and continuous training of the mind will pave the path to ultimate success.

Do not fall prey to the dictates of your mind!

Optimistic, heroic and noble ideals have a powerful and uplifting effect upon the body. Enthusiasm with deliberate well-orchestrated self-application in joyous mood and absolute optimism is the secret path to wealth for all great men.

The preceding chapter highlighted the importance of cultivating correct attitude and developing faith in what you seek to achieve in life.

Nothing in life is impossible, unless you think it so. Thoughts are remarkable 'packets' of energy and if you tenaciously cling to a certain thought with the dynamic willpower, there is no reason why this thought cannot manifest according to the blueprint you have created.

Earlier I briefly mentioned by explaining how a person interested in art can step up his/her abilities to excel in life. I shall now use the same example to illustrate the power of thought. An artist develops an idea of creating a painting or a drawing of a beautiful landscape.

The thought process initiates a series of ideas and the artist subsequently uses these ideas to produce the skeleton work, which allows him/her to eventually complete the final work of art according to the mental blueprint created initially. A mere thought process allows the artist to create the masterpiece!

This creation is in itself a scientific principal based on the Universal Law Of Creation. It is the source from which everything manifests. It is in us all, and it can certainly be tapped if you are just willing to give it a go. The secret is not really a secret, but it is a treasure trove within each and every one of us and we have the right to use it most efficaciously.

Is it not true that when you see someone so very happy and elated, your mind gets caught up with the cheer and you discover that there is a smile on your face?

The thoughts are so closely interweaved with the mind. If the thoughts are calm the mind is calm. In any aspect of life, be it starting a business, getting your first job or getting married, the relationship of mind and thought is foremost.

Systematically, therefore we must train and discipline the mind for right thinking and diligent activity, and thus have correct understanding of what you really want in life, and how this will add to the effectual dynamism in your quest and what you ultimately seek – your path to success and wealth will become gracious, meaningful and attainable!

People with certain qualities are almost magnetically attracted, and such qualities are called positive qualities. These qualities are present in all of us, but they are not invoked or clearly understood. We know what love, kindness, courage and joy mean, these are noble virtues, and we also recognize them as qualities we admire in others.

Despite knowing this, when we act we act compromising ideals. The reason behind this is that we are never true to our own selves – we are constantly acting and putting up a 'show' to please everyone around us, but ourselves! It is painful, demoralizing and quite agonizing not to be your true self.

You may exclaim in disbelief, and sat what has this got to do with wealth and prosperity? I acknowledge your concern, but I humbly request that you take a moment or two, and in the silence of the night ruminate over this point deeply. I would like you then to implement what I mentioned above by being **yourself.**

Notice the changes that occur with the passage of time, and what you will truly discover is that when one can bring out into expression the fragrance of one's innate positive qualities or characteristics (of who you really are), then not only people but all the things that you have ever desired or wished for will come to you.

"As the thought, so the mind."

In order to fulfill your set goals and your dreams, it is necessary to practice what the book outlines.

The habitual inclination of our thought patterns is ultimately the deciding factor, which determines our abilities, talents and our personal characteristics. Based on this critical and vital piece of knowledge, one assumes that those lucky few have been born with the special talent you lack and fervently desire to have.

To a large extent this is true, but it has to be said that no one is born a millionaire – full stop! The valuable information lies in the art of cultivating the pattern that brings success. We are what we think we are.

It is true when Masters say that, "Your Thoughts create the environment".

- Thoughts develop personality
- Thoughts promote health
- Thoughts influence the body
- Thoughts can change and shape the future (destiny)
- Thoughts bring forth creation
- Thoughts influence the physiology and psychology of people
- Thoughts can bring success
- Thoughts can even heal the body

Watch your thoughts constantly. Your experiences and the environment have their 'seat' in thoughts.

Your suggestion, and autosuggestions via meditation and visualization techniques must be stronger than the 'thoughts, and when your actions uplift you, know that you have understood the art of controlling your thought processes.

You can accomplish anything through the power of thought. Visualization uses your imagination to allow yourself to 'picture' your success or achieving your earnest goal.

Your mental thoughts or vibrations are incredibly powerful, because the mind has a tangible connection with your thoughts and your actions. Your thoughts are subtle energies and have a strong connection to our consciousness.

Therefore, constant nourishment of positive thoughts via visualization, yoga and meditation will bring harmony, happiness, health and wealth!

Factors That Bring Inertia

First and foremost is to introspect, and this literally means that you take stock of your traits and habits.

Often, lack of self-analysis is the cause of our short fall, and it is the lack of definite, undivided effort and attention that stands in your way to progress and achievement of your desired goal.

Introspection therefore means reassessment of our mental 'block' and diagnosing deficiencies by weeding out negative tendencies in the form of habits, indecisiveness, fear, lack of confidence and so on – what we often term as failures.

It is time to reenergize so that by uprooting all these negativities from your life the true happiness with the zeal to progress becomes prominent and firmly rooted.

The greatest enemy that stops us from advancing in life other than apathy, lack of confidence and inferiority complex is **FEAR.** Fear will literally stop us from moving forward – in fact we will not even fulfill our very aim to succeed. The best way to combat fear is to practice deep breathing exercises, and every night mentally affirm that you are under the protection of the supreme personality of godhead, and energize your thoughts with positive feelings.

Consciously uproot the seeds of fear from within by forceful concentration upon courage, and shift your awareness to a level that allows you to fully appreciate that you are beyond any type or kind of hurting. Fear comes from the heart, so fill your heart with LOVE, and when you feel agitated relax, calm down and breathe rhythmically, relaxing with each exhalation.

Of course there is yet another problem, which I believe, is the major cause of frustration and subsequently dampening our ability to excel in life. It is, what I call 'desirous of results without the will to put in the effort'. I have personally failed because of such a negative outlook – and I am the first one to admit this openly.

Now this is where the point I made above becomes clearer. Failure, sorrow, illness and inadequacies are natural eventualities when the Law of Nature is broken.

Transgression and violation of the eternal Law of nature brings misery. As human beings we have the abilities to shape, correct and change our lives, goals and destiny.

The greatest impediment that you will ever meet in your life is your immediate environment. If anything you will have to change that – you may have noticed that I started this book sounding slightly cynical and somewhat over cautious, much less a little negative – the prime reason for this will now become apparent.

The environment that I just mentioned can be defined into two, namely the inner and the outer. It is these two fields of environment that you will have to watch out for.

All your experiences come from your mind stuff – or the inner environment (thoughts). What you perceive through all your senses from the outside will equally shape your future.

Thus the important point here is to keep watch over your thoughts. My suggestion to you is to beware of your inner environment more so than your outer environment. For example you may have stumbled upon a great home business opportunity that is potentially superb and just right for you in every aspect.

You are happy, and quite willing to give it a go…yet in retrospect something about this business 'stops' you from going ahead with it. There may be several reasons for this, but I am very curious to learn the major reason. Rest assured it cannot be the money (because it is within your budget), nor can it be a hype (because it has apparently worked for thousands with testimonials to confirm).

So what is it I wonder? Think about this point, and you will no doubt come to a favorable conclusion…and surprisingly it is, the mind stuff – the perpetrator.

To succeed in life you will have to begin by correcting your thought patterns, because it is the company of your thoughts and the affinity you have for them that will determine your fate.

"Thoughts express through the physical body."

The Risk Factor

Without digressing from the subject matter, I would like to remind you what I mentioned in the early stages of the book regarding the dualistic nature of life.

Why is it that some people are so lucky and yet others fall behind in the struggle to succeed?

To answer this conclusively it is worth noting that in general majority of people have the notion that affluent people have something special which they obviously lack – This is not true as we all know, however what makes one person richer than the other is largely dependent on the choice or the decision taken, coupled with the risk(s) acknowledged through the greater understanding of the power of discrimination, and the ability to weigh and balance the scales of your intuitive faculty.

Now the risk that you take has got to be one based on the understanding that the venture you have decided to pursue has been researched thoroughly. You only embark upon taking a driving test for example once you feel that you are proficient enough to pass it and not otherwise.

Thus, the risk that you undertake in this regard has got to be what I call an informed risk. In other words, it is one where you have confidence on what you are getting yourself into, and this too is based on information source that you have searched well.

The fact that you are now reading this report is to gain the understanding on how to achieve financial success – thus this report is in a way your research tool to enable you to then implement the techniques and the tips outlined to achieve the goal. The action taken has therefore come directly from a source that can be considered authentic, valuable and genuine.

Once you feel confident to take the driving test with the guidance of the driving instructor of course, you decide to take the driving test – this is the perfect way to ensure success. I wish to redress a point made previously and it is about learning.

You must be willing to learn constantly, because to gain any skill, knowledge and power, you must be prepared to LEARN.

Commitment is the vital force which you should very much get used to from the very onset. Remember that there are certain situations that you may not have direct control to bring any foreseeable changes, which may result in much heartache.

However, this need not ever be the case because what really matters is the mechanism or the manner in which you control the situation and ultimately how well you react to it.

The trouble with us is that we tend to live in the past and in the future at the same time. When our mental faculty becomes over burdened we become discouraged.

The load is too heavy for the mind, so we must restrict the load. When we have too much to do at one time, we should at once stop our activities. The clock ticks on at a regular pace, it cannot tick twenty four hours away in 60 seconds, nor can you do in one hour what you can do most effectively in twenty four hours. Live for the now, and the 'future' will take care of itself.

Do not be greedy and above all do not burn yourself out by 'wanting' to become a millionaire!

The tables have turned around, more and more people are resorting to a simple back to basics lifestyle – without so many luxuries and fewer worries.

The dualistic concept of nature is prevalent everywhere – you cannot prosper if you write out checks without having credible funds or credit (deposit) in your bank account, sooner or later you will run out of money.

Without peace of mind, you more than likely to run out of 'steam', happiness, calmness and strength. You will become 'bankrupt' mentally, emotionally, spiritually and physically drained. What a pity it will have all been to come to a point of utter desolation!

This is when you must dwell on the power within, and mentally affirm your purpose in life. You may want to go through some pleasant experiences so that you forget your worries completely. The point is do not take anything too seriously, enjoy what you have and be happy with what is due to you.

What You Must Avoid

It is natural that when the unforeseen happens we are far more likely to react in a negative way. However, this need not be so, this book will reveal ways to achieve your goal harmoniously and diligently.

The following are some pointers that will be most helpful:

1. When things go wrong do not overreact. Think positively and calmly.

2. Do not be over judgmental, and over critical.

3. Try not to ignore a bad situation, beware of the comfort zone.

4. Wisdom and strength alone can help you overcome much of life's imminent problems.

5. Tackle problems head on.

6. Avoid greed and conceit of any kind.

There is a business ethic, and a businessman should practice this ethic. Those who are strictly honest and truthful will flourish in business. Let us once again consider art as an example to highlight what has been discussed thus far. As we all know, we have innate powers. Within each and every one of us lies the storehouse of latent energy waiting to be 'awakened'.

Let us assume that you have the creative power and that being an artist for example you can virtually paint and draw any subject or theme.

Fair enough, it is obvious that you have considerable talent as not all artists have this ability. Since you are aware of this, you may assume that because your artwork is good it has good potential to be sold. True, but let us consider all factors that need to be taken into account a step at a time.

1. You may be a very good artist, but if your work does not get noticed and appreciated, it is of no real benefit. It is important therefore that your work gets noticed (through maximum exposure) and the way to do this is get your name established.

This requires that you contact the right sources and approach artists who have been through the 'same' learning curve as it were to reach the path of prosperity. You must take into consideration competition that may exist in your chosen field. You must prepare a good foundation – this can be done using the information within the pages of this book.

2. Your artwork may be exceptionally beautiful, but without understanding the dynamics of the market place your work may not blossom.

3. From your personal perspective your work may seem to have great potential. However, it is relevant to appreciate the views of the general public – in other words your potential buyers.

Do not get into the rut that most do, "hearing what we want to hear" this is a type of preconditioning that can bring untold misery.

4. You must look into other areas to develop your potential. Expand on subject category/theme, use of various different types of media (e.g. acrylics, oils. Mixed media etc.), deciding on how to promote your work, you may even want to sell originals or reproduce prints perhaps… The possibilities are endless, the question is how determined you are in your quest to succeed.

The psychology of success depends on number of factors, but the one I believe that is most vital is self-belief. Most people never get the first stage of success because they lack this characteristic, which is essential.

Such conditioning often stems from your personal experiences, but the causative factor is environment, which has already been discussed. Though it is good to be cautious about anything that you do in life, it is equally essential that you do not get tangled into the technicalities of the 'process', but rather focus on the benefits and the ultimate reward that it yields.

Dedicate your goal to achieving success by implementing the five cardinal words beginning with the letter D to your success, namely Devotion, Discrimination, Discipline, Determination and Duty.

There is no harm in raising questions regarding proposals that come your way or even business opportunities you intend pursuing. So long as these questions afford all the answers and that you decide to follow through considering all the factors, then it is all well and good.

However, when your questions defeat the very purpose of your inquiry then it becomes a 'vicious cycle'.

Why, what, where, when, who are words that we often use to ascertain information about everything in life including business ventures – thus giving rise to questions.

The question with the word why is a necessity for it will help us draw a perfect conclusion and help us overcome doubts. The problem with this is that if you are not clear about your goal(s), then the very question why you wish to even pursue the venture becomes meaningless.

What you must consider are probable long-term goals, benefits and how your first step to wealth and success will enable you to enjoy greater heights.

The Inevitable Mistakes

As human beings we are very restless – we often become overwhelmed with joy, success or gratification. It is so very important to maintain your calm during such events, because excitement can lead to problems, of which one is over spending.

That said, it is also quite important to realize that success may just 'knock' you back, in that you may become complacent and 'decide' not to do much, because you 'have it all'.

This is a terrible phase that you could ever possibly get into, and one you must consciously be aware of at all times. However, the one thing that you must beware of is the ego complex – do not let your ego become an impediment in your endeavor to attain wealth.

The best medicine to avoid ego is to conserve energy. The energy that has been generated and conserved, unless it is directed into the right channels, it will be catastrophic.

We must control our urges, and this is where the art of practicing balance in life becomes an essential tool to your success. Idle talk is one single factor that can destroy your desire to succeed.

Remember, that people around you and the company you have will determine your future success – you may waste precious time, but those around you will make it even worse, they will contribute to overall wastage of your own time.

Thus as the saying goes, 'like attracts like' should be the maxim, and above all use your common sense at all times, and only do that which produces positive results.

Being systematic too will help avoid confusion and annoyances, which can both, have an adverse effect in your business venture and goals. Do not take on board work that may set you back.

Try to evaluate the situation, paying much importance on priorities – do not procrastinate, do not waste time and most of all do not waste your precious energy. If you act thoughtfully your time will be managed most efficiently.

If words, deeds, thoughts and actions are good then life will be good. Each moment will bring success and 'time' taken to achieve the coveted goal will be…well your guess is as good as mine.

"Mind is the cause for bondage and freedom."

Simply by understanding common principles, of which some have already been discussed above, one can attain success.

A conscious effort has to be made to provide good experiences for the mind. Nature has provided man with everything in vast abundance – sadly though human beings have not quite realized this fact.

You must make up your mind to be successful. How can you do this effectively?

How can you develop will? Success comes with planning, determination and faith no doubt. To ascertain this fact I suggest that you try the following: Choose an objective that you think you cannot accomplish, and then try with all your energy and strength to do that one thing.

This could be anything, from drawing a portrait to mastering how to use the computer. When you have achieved success, go on to something bigger and continue striving forward exercising your willpower. Despite any setbacks do not be shaken at all, but derive strength from your surroundings and above all learn from like-minded people who have sought to achieve success courageously without ever losing hope.

Remind yourselves of people like Abraham Lincoln, Henry Ford, Ben Carson, William Cardozo, Mother Teresa and many more who have achieved the coveted positions', because of their innate power of faith and dynamic willpower. *Remember, you too can achieve the same success.*

This law can be applied by anybody and it works. It is true that our thoughts and actions shape our future and destiny. You must be willing to channel your talent and innate capabilities in the right direction, so that you can soar to new heights.

To recap on what has been said thus far, allow me to remind you what it takes to be successful.

• Planning is crucial and perhaps the most important step to your success.

• Prepare yourself to change your views, habits and your thought patterns.

• Only pursue tasks that are important. You must divide your needs from your wants – there is a fine line, so exercise discrimination.

• Watch your personal financial situation. Budget well and reduce spending.

• Surround yourself with people with a positive persona and those who are successful.   Read books about people who have succeeded in life.

• Do not pretend to be who you are not. Be yourself and do not show off.

• Expand your horizon and be enthusiastic and ambitious.

• It is good to increase your income but it is even better to invest in assets that will make you wealthy.

• Prepare to work hard and make sacrifices.

Right actions enrich, strengthen and motivate us fully vitalizing our inner resources.

Cultivation of such values and adhering to the right values of living will help us grow and achieve success.

Such a consistent regime and exposure can mould our character and will help redeem our lower tendencies.

Time to Learn Who You Are

I would frown upon anyone who would even think of making a comment, by saying that success is only a wishful thought.

We are not born failures – let me get this point straightened. We have all been successful in our lives at some stage or another, and this is an undeniable TRUTH.

The following points will surely enable you to understand who you really are, and that is a guarantee. Once you ascertain your own attributes, it becomes that much easier to embrace ideals that will allow you to leap to greater heights.

1. Are you generally enthusiastic and positive or the complete opposite?

2. Do you like to work hard and would you put in that little bit of extra effort if you did what you love most?

3. Are you being all that you can be – you may want to analyze your strengths and weaknesses.

4. Are you content with your present situation and/or circumstances?
Upon answering these three very important issues, you can determine your future. Remind yourselves about the importance of discipline and organization mentioned earlier.

The next point I wish to highlight is simplicity. Do not unnecessarily create hardships in the way of your work and the goal to success.

By simplicity I mean, do not complicate situation, and do not let success get to your head – pompous attitude is yet another problem that may bring you down. Be humble, assertive and righteous in your endeavors to succeed.

A calm individual can achieve virtually anything simply through the power of concentration – this is a scientific based truth.

Research has clearly shown that techniques like yoga, visualization, and relaxation can bring heightened awareness, thereby allowing the individual to reach his maximum potential.

By the power of concentration and focus, a person can accomplish that which he/she has desired.

The Need for Change

We are all too aware that nothing ever remains permanent in life, despite understanding one fact that life itself is a continuum, what we have failed to realize is that our own attitudes, conditioning and propensities stops us from incorporating changes.

One of the most difficult things to change is our nature (the indelible thoughts), particularly those that have left a mark (blueprint) on our psyche.

We may be able to change a lot of things around us but the need to change our thoughts, attitudes and habits which almost certainly have become a part of our self identity becomes arduously difficult a task.

As with all things in life, time can heal anything and everything. Allow time to help you grow in life and without wasting time reach your individual goals.

How do we change our mental attitude? The answer is very easy – once again there is no secret as such, nor is this arduous a task to implement. The primary answer lies in the word change itself. Initiating gradual changes in your lifestyle will help you reach your goal much faster. I say that the answer is easy with respect to how we can bring about positive changes, because let us consider habits for instance.

Habits take time to take root, as we are all too aware. Just as you 'learn' your habits with time you simply begin to unlearn them. Habits are very difficult to eradicate at once, and thus you allow time to take care of your habits. What has this got to do with being happy and rich, I 'hear' you ask?

Well, my friends I would like to throw back the very same question to you! Ask yourself why you have not been able to progress?

Put into practice what you have gathered thus far. Sit in a quiet corner and open your heart out, and solve this problem – the answer to all you problems, good or bad lie within you. The exactness of the problem will no doubt vary, but the reason(s) for it are self-explanatory.

They stem from experiences, environment and your thought patterns. Why is it that person Y is able to quit smoking and yet person Z has much difficulties to quit the habit, though both have been smoking for ten years, and both smoke twenty cigarettes a day? The answer lies in what I have already discussed above, and it is our THOUGHTS.

The primary things that you will have to change in your life is your current perception of who you are, what others think of you and finally, who you really are?

While you can change your thoughts, your environment and your business strategies, what you will have to realize is that you will not be able to change the very Law of Nature – it is perfect. Thus, we must respect this and begin to adhere to its governing dynamics, without violating it. How can nature affect our success?

This is a valid question, but upon deep analysis you will understand that we as human beings are constantly breaking the rules, laws and life's eternal processes daily.

Without digressing from the subject matter too much, carefully watch and notice how the beautiful rhythm of nature is fulfilling its duty daily without any discordance, and interruption. Likewise we have a lot to learn from Nature. Deviation from truth leads to utter dismay and failure, and breaking the Laws of Nature will bring despair – in short the macrocosm and the microcosm are indifferent.

The decisions that you make in your life will determine the outcome of your future events. Always think first of what you are about to do or intend on doing, and by undertaking this act how will it then affect you. This is the Law of Cause and Effect.

Do not act on impulse, but rather remain calm, quiet and try to maintain deep silence as much as you can. It is simply amazing what you can achieve through silence and introspection.

I do suggest that you undertake a form of relaxation exercise, such as meditation or even yoga to help you achieve peace and success. Good judgment is a perfect indicator of wisdom through the expression of the power of intellect via the discriminative faculty.

If you have clearly recognized your folly, then you must admit mistakes and bad habits. If it annoys others or affects your health, conscience, financial status, family, well-being and your peace of mind, then you must ask, 'How much better off would I be without it?' If you do not benefit from this – why even take it up or think about it?

Understanding Failure

'Reason is the greatest enemy that faith has.'

This is a fact because both the believer and the non-believer are quite likely to resort to this statement in support of their respective arguments.

You have already been acquainted to life's dualistic nature, and as such human reason will find both 'pros' and cons' for both good and bad action respectively.

This is when you have to learn to be guided by the inner voice of 'conscience'. *The following arise from this innate powerhouse, intuition, truth, peace, righteousness, love, nonviolence (in words, deeds, actions and thoughts) and power of discrimination. These attributes have their existence in the soul.*

This is the greatest truth that you cannot afford not to know. Effort is proportional to grace, but I wish to add that success is proportional to effort only when you have learned to appreciate the qualities of love.

Whatever you do put in all your effort and do whatever you do with absolute love.

Those who are willing to take risks achieve success. It is a known fact, that young people are more adaptable to changes. As we age it becomes a little tricky and tougher to bring about changes and the ability to adapt to wide ranging comfort zones. Before it becomes too late, weed out the problem early on – do not allow it to gnaw into your system. Like a virus take action and remove it from your system at once.

The fact is that we are born perfect (I do not mean this in a physical sense of the word), but the rigors of time 'adulterates' this perfection, and therefore the infinite possibilities that lie lurking within us become diffused.

However, what makes us superior is that there is but one great and covetable gift which is ours all the time. This is our extraordinary power to discover, develop and declare that we as human beings have the capacity to reach great if not greater heights. Lying within us is the infinite source of energy that is distinctly ours!

Most people as I am sure you will agree, do everything half-heartedly, and the reasons(s) for this have all been covered.

They do not use their full potential, mainly because they have not understood the power of the mind.

Often we are drawn or compelled to do things that bring sorrow. Temporary pleasures bring sorrow, and consequently majority of us through fear or perhaps even lack of confidence are 'forced' to throw in the white towel.

This need not be the case, because this book gives you the ability to overcome these hurdles, by delivering words so potent that you can change your circumstances. It is high time that you watch the graphs of your mind very carefully.

Upon introspection it is now time to weed out the dirt and through the use of the power of discrimination distinguish that which gives you lasting happiness as opposed to sorrow.

The bottom line is you have to exercise control over your thoughts.

The following is included to guide you to your journey to wealth, health and happiness.

• Avoid dwelling on all the wrongs things you have done.

• Repeating wrong actions over and over become habits. Simply take care not to repeat those actions again.

• Do not think of yourself as a failure. Use failures as a means to acquiring success – do not give up until you reach your desired goal.

• You will have to erase the grooves of bad habits that you have created by creating good habits. If you are lazy decide to become positively active and assertive – set yourself tasks or goals and make sure you achieve them.

The fact that we resist change shows that we have our own 'comfort zones' and this is a result of our thoughts. Why is it that we resist change? The simple answer to this question is fear of change.

A change means that we have to let go of that which we 'feel' is 'right' for us.

The question then remains to be asked is what is right for you? This is a difficult one, and the answer is that until we are not fully content within ourselves then even a millionaire who desires an extra million is a beggar. How many of us are content?

We seek instant results, and when we do not 'see' results we become despondent and subsequently give up. It is my belief that when you desire a thing for the right reasons then nothing will ever stop you from acquiring it – this is the eternal law.

Paving Your Path to Success

I wrote this book with only one intention in mind and that is to help you understand and ultimately help you realize the Power of the Mind.

What you will shortly find out is a series of steps that you have to follow very strictly to ascertain your deep-seated desire. These steps are not monumental tasks, but simple guidelines to get you started.

1. Believe in yourself, and the power of affirmations. Successful people become successful through constant use of their willpower. Do not be frightened of mishaps in the initial stages. Transform failures into success through wisdom, strength and faith.

2. Believe in the philosophy of 'simple living and high thinking'.

3. Do not hold anything against anyone. Strive to overcome your past grievances and move on. Try to forgive everybody 'hurt never help ever'.

4. Honesty is the golden rule. Observe silence, meditate and remove all negative tendencies from your system (i.e. jealousy, ego, hatred, fear and so on). Stick to the following principles, love, truth, righteousness, peace and non-violence (you must not even injure anyone through your speech, actions and thoughts).

With absolute determination, it is relevant that to acquire success you associate with people who have already attained it.

To appreciate the purpose of this book, it becomes vitally important to scrutinize the following points. It will make more sense to you now, why success or failure depends on how you define yourself:

IMAGE: The better you feel about your self-image the more likely you will succeed. Image does not necessarily mean looks; it also has a deeper meaning and connotes reflection.

The image that you may have about yourself is more likely to stem from what you 'think' about yourself. The internal environment that I have discussed earlier can play a crucial role in determining your final goal.

EMOTIONS: It is obvious that our thoughts and feelings, which are subtle, have tremendous influence in our lives. The best way to counteract these subtle forces is to exercise silence during meditation and relaxation exercises.

It is advisable to take up a form of exercise to keep your mind positively active. Of course the second benefit is health. Healthy body serves as a perfect 'vehicle' to do well.

Every individual seeks happiness in life. Now the very happiness we seek becomes a joy once found. This joy can surmount to 'bliss' simply by incorporating.

LOVE. You must share love in what you do and you must love what you accomplish daily in your life. In the silence of the night, introspect and learn how to improve your life (in words, deeds, thoughts and actions) and thank the supreme universal energy.

Together with what has been said above, good communication skills, interaction and good relationship is the way ahead – this is ultimately the essence of fine virtues and character that will make you successful.

Develop a harmonious personality, and remember what was mentioned at the start, always use loving words – words can bring peace or start a world war.

Conditioning your mind effectively will allow you to reap the rewards. It is very good practice to scrutinize your daily thoughts just prior to bedtime, and log this in your progress book.

Set goals and targets daily and work at it until you achieve them.

Time is the most precious asset in life, use it wisely – time wasted is life wasted. When you decide to achieve success in your life, make sure you do not have conflicting thoughts. If you learn how to consciously control and thus implement the inexhaustible powers within you, you can accomplish much more.

Language is nothing but the expression of thoughts and experiences. Communication plays a vital role in your overall success, much less your day-to-day living. Through the power of knowledge, you can achieve specific goals, because the secret of our strength is in our knowledge. When you have an idea that is workable it is necessary to focus on it hundred percent.

Do not tell the world about it – there is no need for such 'show'. Ponder over it and develop it into a 'product' that has a sound base. Without a firm foundation an edifice has no chance to stand.

The Law of Prosperity

There is no harm to desire success and all the other good things in life, but rest assured, desire which leads to the nagging feeling of lack or incompleteness can be dangerous.

If for any reason desire leads to sleepless nights and frustration - it is time to STOP whatever it is that you are doing.

This brings me to a tale by an unknown author in which I have used to author my Quest in life. It is called, "The Tale of The American Businessman and The Mexican Fisherman."

An American businessman was standing at the pier of a small coastal Mexican village when a small boat with just one fisherman docked. Inside the small boat were several large yellow fin tuna. The American complimented the Mexican on the quality of his fish.

"How long did it take you to catch them?" the American asked.

"Only a little while," the Mexican replied.

"Why don't you stay out longer and catch more fish?" The American asked.

"I have enough to support my family's immediate needs," the Mexican said.

"But," the American then asked, "What do you do with the rest of your time?"

The Mexican fisherman said, "I sleep late, fish a little, play with my children, take a siesta with my wife, and stroll into the village each evening where I sip wine and play guitar with my amigos. I have a full and busy life, señor."

The American scoffed, "I am a Harvard MBA and could help you. You should spend more time fishing and with the proceeds you can buy a bigger boat, and with the proceeds from the bigger boat you could buy several boats. Eventually you would have a fleet of fishing boats."

The American continued, "Instead of selling your catch to a middleman you would sell directly to the consumers, eventually opening your own can factory. You would control the product, processing and distribution. You would need to leave this small coastal village and move to Mexico City and eventually New York where you will run your expanding enterprise."

The Mexican fisherman asked, "But señor, how long will all of this take?"

The American replied, "15-20 years."

"Then what, señor?"

The American laughed and said, "That's the best part. When the time is right you would announce an IPO (Initial Public Offering) and sell your company stock to the public and become very rich. You will make millions."

"Millions, señor? Then what?"

The American said slowly, "Then you would retire. You would move to a small coastal fishing village where you would sleep late, fish a little, play with your kids, take a siesta with your wife, and stroll into the village each evening where you could sip wine and play your guitar with your amigos…"

This story is my inspiration and it's moral is to slow down and take a real look at what is important to you and how you really aspire to live. Often times we chase more, and sometimes we fail to see that we may already BE where we are trying so hard to GET.

Contentment is the true single factor of affirming your abundance. A selfish desire leads to utter failure!

Spiritual law is very powerful indeed.

That said, you must endeavor to follow the following principles daily in your life. Always be good to all around you, do not be treacherous and deceitful. Beware of the ego and be true and sincere.

Thoughtfulness is incredibly important, so always remind yourself of people who may not be so lucky, and extend your helping hand as much as you possibly can to those who deserve it.

Training your mind to accomplish great heights is not a difficult task. In your spare time, do not waste your energy; instead spend time contemplating on the power of your innate being.

Meditate daily and visualize your success and your goals. My friends, the power of the mind is simply awesome, the fact is that we do not even use 10 percent of it in our daily lives. Now based on this scientific understanding just imagine what you could achieve if you were to use the remaining 90 percent?

Just as you savor food when you chew it and taste it – perform each and every act with a sense of gratitude and do it willingly and most importantly happily.

Do NOT follow every little impulse blindly, learn to reflect and distinguish between what is temporary and fleeting and what is lasting, what is essential and what is non essential, between what is pleasing and what is unworthy.

Self-conquest will give us that which we are seeking. It has to be stressed that balance is also an essential ingredient in your quest for success and wealth. You must allocate time for yourself and your family or the loved one's. A permanent happiness must be independent of a changing environment.

Do not become a workaholic or a 'wealthaholic' freak in your quest to success, lest it damages your relationship, much less your attempts to sincerely succeed in life.

Do not deviate from the path of righteousness or the Law of Nature. It is great fun indeed to witness success and wealth, and the joy that wells up is beyond belief no doubt. However, if happiness, joy and success all come at once at the expense of your health, then I am afraid it is all a terrible waste.

The way to being wealthy, is by the employment of the following virtues which is our real true nature, and it is to be found not just in human beings but everything around you: Truth, righteousness, peace, love and non violence. Ask yourself, that if all fellow human beings apply these attributes consistently – the world and its inhabitants would prosper.

We must approach all our work (including problems) or duties with concentrated energy and thus execute it with absolute perfection. Endeavor to do all the things (little or however small a duty or job this may be) in an extraordinary way. Perform all your work and duty with LOVE and enthusiasm, and watch the results. Never attempt anything half heartedly; you will not progress in life.

Power of Words

Power of words can have a very strong impact on our minds and in our lives.

Before I continue, I would like you to cogitate on the following question, could someone remain silent at all times?

Not letting anyone know what is inside his/her heart and mind for the mere reason of not being verbally or emotionally expressive? Yet I can say with certainty that each and every one of us are silent talkers. We talk to ourselves in many ways and situations, sometimes we hurt ourselves and yet at other times, silent talking brings a wonderful smile to our faces!

Communication is therefore very important in life. Words are powerful and depending on how they are spoken, they can influence our day-to-day thought processes, actions, behavior and our outlook towards life as a whole.

42

Of course depending on how they are used the effect words can have is quite incredible, they can be used to persuade, inform, hurt, ease pain or even start a war! Words spoken with great emotions have the power to bring changes that can speed up the body's healing process!

This enormous power is in the meaning of the words, what they mean to the person who hears them. Far more than simple communication, truth, falsehood and the infinite shades between them. Words have the power to manipulate other people's thinking and behavior.

It is our interpretation of words that is the true cause of our emotional reactions.

Words spoken softly, unselfishly, innocently and with absolute love are the ones that get lodged indelibly in our being from whence they produce their overwhelming soul stirring effect. Thus it is so important to use words selectively and appropriately at any given time and situation.

Modern science is beginning to appreciate the powerful effect words can have on our bodies when they are used in the form of prayers or even affirmations. Did you know that through conscious effort, we could create a very strong willpower in ourselves?

Affirmation for success:

I will pursue relentlessly, as it is my birthright to be successful. I am powerful and I shall achieve what I need at the time I need. I am destined to reap the fruits of my actions and I will share my joy in success with all I know.

Benefits of Affirmations

- Self-esteem and a positive outlook
- Helps you achieve goals and targets
- Improve your memory and skills
- Helps to create an inner self-belief (willpower, confidence and character)
- It can help you evolve spiritually

Words spoken softly gently and lovingly will be attractive and procure instant admiration. Wealth is in itself a word, and by itself it does not mean anything.

The one single factor, which gives the word wealth, the meaning is the intellect. The wealth of information is nowhere to be found, but it is within us at all times. Intellect is cultivated through logic, and the main point is that dry logic and philosophy can often prove counterproductive. Thus, it is essential to communicate effectively, because in pursuit of wealth, you will need to sell yourself your business or your company via communication (words).

However, communication on its own will not reciprocate your success.

The Power of Unconditional Love

It seems to me that people have forgotten the real value, meaning and definition of the word love.

You may exclaim and say what has love got to do with wealth! It is naturally difficult to define true love, let me explain, say you want to learn how to swim, you read books about the art of becoming a good swimmer, but until you jump into the swimming pool under guidance, the true meaning of swimming does not have any real value or meaning.

You will have to taste the fruit to know its real flavor, as the saying goes.

Selfish loves rooted in desires that are in no way harmonious is the most damaging, and if you become 'immersed' in acquiring your goals via deception, calumny and against all the noble and ethical principles than you might as well put this book away.

Those who understand love live in harmony and it is natural that these individuals will attract what they have willed to achieve.

The greatest power of attraction in every sense of the word be it a relationship, business and friendship is love.

As a budding entrepreneur, remember that the attractive power of love is incredible – you must practice compassion, and watch yourself grow and watch your venture thrive.

Upon achieving any form of success in life it becomes pertinent that no matter what happens, you do not force your success on anybody – avoid egoism, pride and do not impose your power on anyone – it is wrong to do so.

It is crucial that by getting wealthy, you do not abuse your newly acquired 'power'. When power is used appropriately know that you have achieved glory.

Conclusion

This book is written with the view to allow you to discern the innate latent powers that lie dormant within each and every one of us.

Opportunity seekers cannot really afford to 'chose and pick', but rather they should learn to capitalize on every bit of chance that is afforded to them.

As a seeker avail yourself to opportunities that have the potential to become indispensable gateway to success. It is all about taking calculated, controlled, measured and an informed risk.

Wealthy individuals have created their own career because they are true believers of success.

These are individuals who cannot stop until they achieve success. They become rebellious fighters only to earn their unflinching goal. They are disciplined warriors wielding their weapons of truth, honesty, sincerity, compassion, determination, power, principles, righteousness, wisdom, faith, self-belief, creativity, fortitude and prowess to reach heights par excellence.

Life functions strictly according to the natures incorrigible laws. The reason for this is to establish efficiency, and within the ambit of law, the rational intellect in man can be developed to a greater efficiency.

You are wealthy already, however due to the lack of understanding your powerful innate qualities, these attributes lying in abundance have not found the dynamism to express and manifest.

Finally do not take life too seriously. Life is a journey made possible for us all, and if we are willing to give ourselves the opportunity to grow, then life can be so wonderfully experienced. It is most entertaining, especially when one follows its governing principles religiously.

State of complete tranquility is possible and there is mounting proof to establish the greatness achieved by common people throughout history. It is time that you employ the powers of your mind to achieve your desire(s).

Be happy at all times, when difficulties arise, laugh at them, and employ the dynamic willpower within you to fight them off. As mentioned elsewhere, the body and especially the mind is truly an amazing instrument we have.

www.ingramcontent.com/pod-product-compliance
Lightning Source LLC
Chambersburg PA
CBHW071543170526
45166CB00004B/1532